Spiritual Warfare Prayer Journal

A 50 Week Guided Christian Devotional for Declarations, Decrees, Petition and Thanksgiving

Elizabeth Sang

All rights reserved © 2023, Elizabeth Sang.

No part of this book may be reproduced, or transmitted for commercial purposes in any form or by any means without express written permission of the publisher or author.

Scripture quotations marked (NKJV) are taken from the New King James Version®. Copyright © 1982 by Thomas Nelson. Used by permission. All rights reserved.

Scripture quotations marked (NIV) are taken from the Holy Bible, New International Version®, NIV®. Copyright © 1973, 1978, 1984, 2011 by Biblica, Inc.™ Used by permission of Zondervan. All rights reserved worldwide. www.zondervan.com The "NIV" and "New International Version" are trademarks registered in the United States Patent and Trademark Office by Biblica, Inc.™

Scripture quotations marked (AMP) are taken from the Amplified Bible, Copyright © 2015 by The Lockman Foundation. Used by permission.

"Scripture quotations marked (AMPC) are taken from the Amplified® Bible (AMPC),
Copyright © 1954, 1958, 1962, 1964, 1965, 1987 by The Lockman Foundation

Scripture quotations marked (NASB) are taken from the (NASB®) New American Standard Bible®, Copyright © 1960, 1971, 1977, 1995, 2020 by The Lockman Foundation. Used by permission. All rights reserved. lockman.org"

Scripture quotations marked (ICB) are taken from the International Children's Bible®. Copyright © 1986, 1988, 1999 by Thomas Nelson. Used by permission. All rights reserved.

Scripture quotations marked (NIrV) are taken from the Holy Bible, New International Reader's Version®, NIrV® Copyright © 1995, 1996, 1998, 2014 by Biblica, Inc.™ Used by permission of Zondervan. All rights reserved worldwide. www.zondervan.comThe "NIrV" and "New International Reader's Version" are trademarks registered in the United States Patent and Trademark Office by Biblica, Inc.™

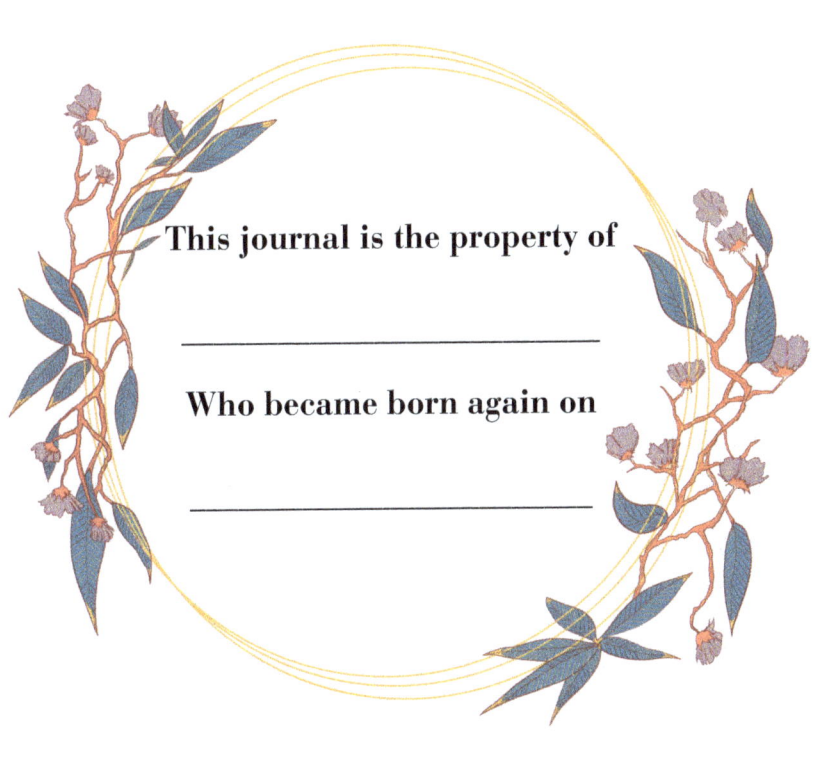

This journal is the property of

_____

Who became born again on

_____

Table of contents

BOOK 1
The Righteous Differ from the Wicked ~ Psalm 1 8
A Morning Prayer of Trusting in God ~ Psalm 3 10
An Evening Prayer for Trusting in God ~ Psalm 4 12
A Prayer for Protection ~ Psalm 5 14
The Lord Defends His Righteous ~ Psalm 7 16
A Prayer for God to Overthrow the Wicked ~ Psalm 10 18
A Prayer for Help when in Trouble ~ Psalm 13 20
Having Hope in the Lord and in His Victory ~ Psalm 16 22
A Prayer for Triumph over Tormentors ~ Psalm 20 24
Jehovah Rohi, My Shepherd ~ Psalm 23 26
The Mighty One in Battle Fights for Me ~ Psalm 35 28
The Lord Himself Upholds the Righteous ~ Psalm 37 30
A Prayer when Suffering Consequences of Sin ~ Psalm 38 32
A Prayer for the Gift of Wisdom ~ Psalm 39 34
Looking up to God for Help ~ Psalm 40 36

BOOK 2
The Lord My Ever-Present Help ~ Psalm 46 38
A Prayer for Pardon from Sin ~ Psalm 51 40
The Lord Faithfully Upholds Me ~ Psalm 54 42
Fully Trusting in God who is Invincible to Man ~ Psalm 56 44
Confidence in the Lord My Refuge ~ Psalm 61 46
A Prayer for Deliverance from Evil Traps and Snares ~ Psalm 64 48
The Favour of the Lord is Abundant ~ Psalm 65 50

BOOK 3
The Results of Wickedness Versus Righteousness ~ Psalm 73 52
The Lord is Glorious in Power ~ Psalm 76 54
The Lord's Victorious Track Record ~ Psalm 77 56
Restore Me O Lord! ~ Psalm 80 58
A Petition to Be Saved from Death ~ Psalm 88 60
A Man After God's Own Heart ~ Psalm 89 62

BOOK 4

God is the Alpha and the Omega ~ Psalm 90 64
The Lord Almighty is My Shelter ~ Psalm 91 66
Praise the Lord for His Lovingkindness ~ Psalm 92 68
Vengeance belongs to the Lord ~ Psalm 94 70
Jehovah, You are the Most High ~ Psalm 97 72
Start with a Grateful Heart ~ Psalm 100 74
The Lord Shall Arise to My Cause ~ Psalm 102 76
The Lord's Everlasting Mercy ~ Psalm 103 78
God's Covenant with Abraham to Generations ~ Psalm 105 80
Man's Rebellion and the Lord's Faithfulness ~ Psalm 106 82

BOOK 5

Thanksgiving for Deliverance ~ Psalm 107 84
Humility Precedes Honour ~ Psalm 113 86
Thanksgiving for Mercy ~ Psalm 118 88
Meditating on the Law of God ~ Psalm 119 90
The Lord is on Guard ~Psalm 121 92
The Lord Provides an Escape ~ Psalm 124 94
True Prosperity is from the Lord ~ Psalm 127 96
Our Omnipresent an Omniscient God Psalm 139 98
A Prayer for Safety from Evil Works ~ Psalm 141 100
A Prayer for Deliverance and Consecration ~ Psalm 143 102
The Lord's Majestic and Loving Nature ~ Psalm 145 104
A Song of Praise to the Lord ~ Psalm 150 106

Hello there!

Thank you for getting your hands on this Spiritual Warfare Prayer Journal. Before you get into it, I would like to offer some guidelines to using it effectively:

- The Journal is based on the Book of Psalms which is a 150-verse, 5-division book in the Bible with various prayers. With the help of the Holy Spirit's revelation, I focused on 50 chapters consisting of prayers & petitions by various Psalmists. You will notice the Psalms start with sorrowful prayers but ends in victorious acclamations. So shall it be in your case in Jesus name!

- The journal consists of 2 pages for every allocated chapter. One page includes quoted and highlighted scripture while the other has 4 sections consisting of insights, declarations & decrees and your own space for prayer requests & note taking or writing your testimonies so you can remember what the Lord has done for you.

- It is a 50 week prayer journal with each chapter selected to meditate on for a week claiming the declarations & decrees over your life every day of the week. As this is written as a prayer journal, you will need to supplement it with a daily devotional or with reading more of your Bible daily to ensure for adequate spiritual nourishment.

- It is important to remember that we fight not against flesh & blood but against principalities, against powers, against the rulers of the darkness of this world, against spiritual wickedness in high places (Ephesians 6:12). So as you pray these prayers don't target specific people as they are only vessels, but rather aim for the principalities acting in & through them. We all have one common enemy as believers of Christ.

- The following will be essential for an effective session when using the prayer journal; your Bible, highlighter, a pen or a pencil & a notebook.

- You can accompany using the journal with one day or more per week of fasting. Make sure you get medical clearance before deciding to fast & allow the Holy Spirit to give you guidance on which day(s) to fast & how many hours you should do it for.

- If led to sow to the ministry for any particular prayers where the Holy Spirit pricks your heart to, please use the QR code to do so. This is located on the last page of this prayer journal. Remember only to do it cheerfully and not by anyone's compulsion as God loves a cheerful giver (2 Corinthians 9:6-7).

- If you want to get contact to share your testimonies so we can thank the Lord with you, reach out to us on theconsecratedministry@gmail.com

- Remember to start every prayer with gratitude, repentance & by inviting your intercessors who for every believer is the Holy Spirit & Jesus Christ.

God bless you!

The Righteous Differ from the Wicked

Psalm 1:6

For the Lord watches over the way of the righteous, but the way of the wicked leads to destruction.
NIV

Also Highlight; Psalm 1:1-3

Date:__/__/____

Insight

Abiding in God & living in accordance to His word makes us fruitful. Unlike the wicked, we are not chaff that is easily blown away by the wind. Instead, we're like trees that grow by streams of water; firmly rooted, unwavering & prosperous.

Prayer Requests

Declare & Decree

1. Lord, engrave Your laws in my heart that I meditate on them day & night.

2. Lord, surround me with people that are of You & for You. May I never compromise my walk with You for this world.

Notes/Testimonies

A Morning Prayer of Gratitude to God

Psalm 3:3

But You, Lord, are a shield around me,
my glory, the One who lifts my head high.
NIV

Also Highlight; Psalm 3:5-6

Date:__/__/____

Insight
God has assured us that He is our shield against the evil in this world. Despite the mockers & scoffers we encounter in our Christian walk, the Lord assures us His defence & sustenance. After all, true & eternal salvation belongs to Him.

Prayer Requests

Declare & Decree
1. Defend me & shield me from my adversaries, Lord. For I look only up to You for Your salvation.
2. I shall not live in fear of those against me but in confidence that the Lord Himself watches over me & sustains me.

Notes/Testimonies

An Evening Prayer of Gratitude to God

Psalm 4:3

*Know that the Lord has set apart his faithful servant for Himself;
the Lord hears when I call to Him.*
NIV

Also Highlight; Psalm 4:4-5

Date:__/__/____

Insight

The Lord has mercy on whom He chooses to have mercy (Exod 33:19; Rom 9:18). God's Omnipotent- all-knowing nature causes Him to discern our hearts & minds. He knows those who are faithful to Him & He listens to them.

Prayer Requests

Declare & Decree

1. Set me apart for Yourself as Your faithful servant Lord, hear me when I call out to You. Choose to have mercy on me!
2. Help me not to sin against You Lord, but to trust in You.
3. Lord, cause the light of Your countenace to shine on me.

Notes/Testimonies

A Prayer for Protection

Psalm 5:12

Surely, Lord, You bless the righteous;
You surround them with Your favour as with a shield.
NIV

Also Highlight; Psalm 5:3 & Psalm 5:11

Date:__/__/____

Insight

Due to God's righteous nature, He will never condone those who take pleasure in wickedness. Jeremiah 17:9 tells us that the heart of man is desperately wicked. But God shows those who put their trust in Him an abundance of love & mercy.

Prayer Requests

Declare & Decree

1. Let me ever sing for joy as I put all my trust & refuge in God.
2. Help me not to sin against You Lord, but to trust in You.
3. Lead me & make Your way straight before me, Lord.
4. Lord, form a shield of favour around me now & forevermore.

Notes/Testimonies

The Lord Defends His Righteous

Psalm 7:8

Let the Lord judge the peoples.
Vindicate me, Lord, according to
my righteousness,
according
to my integrity,
O Most High.
NIV

Also Highlight; Psalm 7:6 & Psalm 7:9

Date:__/__/____

Insight

One of God's names in Hebrew is Jehovah Magen (A shield). He saves those who are upright in their hearts. He is also a righteous judge who discerns the hearts & minds of men. In His might, God saves His righteous & puts an end to the wicked.

Prayer Requests

Declare & Decree

1. O Lord deliver me from the hand of every wicked spirit!
2. O God, arise in Your anger & decree justice on my behalf!
3. Remember my integrity & righteousness and vindicate me!
4. O God, let those who plan evil fall into the pit themselves.

Notes/Testimonies

A Prayer for God to Overthrow the Wicked

Psalm 10:12

Arise, Lord! Lift up Your hand,
O God.
Do not forget the
helpless.
NIV

Also Highlight; Psalm 10:4 & Psalm 10:17-18

Date:__/__/____

Insight

Walking the Christian walk is full of persecution. We expect to face both physical & emotional tribulations while on earth. Evildoers take pride in their oppression of the righteous but God cannot be mocked (Gal 6:7). He is mighty in battle!

Prayer Requests

Declare & Decree

1. Lift up Your hand against my oppressors & silence them Lord!
2. You're a caring & compassionate Father, defend me O Lord!
3. I receive the help of God, my helper in all my battles.
4. O Lord, consider my grief & take it in Your hand.

Notes/Testimonies

A Prayer for Help when in Trouble

Psalm 13:5

But I have trusted and relied on and been confident in Your lovingkindness and faithfulness;
My heart shall rejoice and delight in Your salvation.
AMP

Also Highlight; Psalm 13:3 & Psalm 13:6

Date:__/__/____

Insight

Azariah is a Hebrew name that means 'Yahweh has helped'. We sometimes get impatient in the wait for the Lord's help but our faithful God will always come to our salvation. Even though it tarries, it shall surely come to pass & not be delayed.

Prayer Requests

Declare & Decree

1. From Your throne of grace Lord, see me & remember me.
2. My enemies will never have a reason to rejoice over my case.
3. God is a solid rock in whom I put my confidence in.
4. Lord, deal bountifully with me! Let my harvest overflow!

Notes/Testimonies

Having Hope in the Lord and in His Victory

Psalm 16:5-6

Lord, You alone are my portion and my cup; You make my lot secure. The boundary lines have fallen for me in pleasant places; surely I have a delightful inheritance.
NIV

Also Highlight; Psalm 16:2 & Psalm 16:10-11

Date:__/__/____

Insight

Trusting in God comes with letting go of our own strategies & schemes. 1 Cor. 3:19 tells us that the wisdom of man is but foolishness to God. As the Lord alone is our keeper, we should learn to rest in Him & in the assurance of His protection.

Prayer Requests

Declare & Decree

1. I will delight myself with that which is noble & excellent.
2. The Lord is at my right hand, nothing will shake me.
3. The Faithful & True God will not let me undergo decay.
4. You're my God, & I have no other god beside You.

Notes/Testimonies

A Prayer for Triumph over Tormentors

Psalm 20:7

Some trust in chariots
and some in horses,
but we trust in the name
of the Lord our God.
NIV

Also Highlight; Psalm 20:1-2 & Psalm 20:8

Date:__/__/____

Insight

2 Cor 12:8-10 "My grace is sufficient for you, for My strength is made perfect in weakness." (NKJV) Therefore, we would gladly rather boast in our infirmities, that the power of Christ may rest upon us. He saves by the strength of His righteous right hand.

Prayer Requests

Declare & Decree

1. I receive my strength from Zion today in the name of Jesus!
2. My trust & confidence will always rest in the Lord my God.
3. I will celebrate the joy of my victory in Jesus mighty name!
4. The grace & mercy of God over my life is sufficient.

Notes/Testimonies

Jehovah Rohi, My Shepherd

Psalm 23:4

*Even though I walk
through the darkest valley,
I will fear no evil,
for You are with me;
Your rod and Your staff,
they comfort me.*
NKJV

Also Highlight; Psalm 23:5-6

Date:___/___/____

Insight

Jehovah Rohi is Hebrew for 'The Lord our Shepherd'. Jesus is our good shepherd who lays down His life for His sheep (John 10:11). We can trust in His guidance through the highs & lows of life. As His sheep we're sure His goodness & love will follow us forever.

Prayer Requests

Declare & Decree

1. The Lord will provide for me according to His riches in glory.
2. I will always trust in the Lord's guidance above my own.
3. May my cup always overflow for as long as I abide in Him.
4. I will dwell in the house of the Lord forever Amen!

Notes/Testimonies

The Mighty One in Battle Fights for Me

Psalm 35:1-2

Contend, Lord, with those who contend with me;
fight against those who fight against me.
Take up shield and armour;
arise and come to my aid.
NIV

Also Highlight; Psalm 35:3 & Psalm 35:10

Date:__/__/____

Insight

Our mighty God is El Shaddai meaning 'The Overpowerer. The enemy is stronger than our flesh but not stronger than the Lord & His Holy Spirit. May the God of vengeance pursue every wicked spiritual force pursuing you from high places.

Prayer Requests

Declare & Decree

1. With Your spear & javelin, pursue those who pursue me, Lord!
2. May the angel of the Lord drive to dust all my adversaries!
3. May trap setters fall into the very pit they have set for me!
4. Awake, & rise to my defence! Contend for me, my God!

Notes/Testimonies

The Lord Himself Upholds the Righteous

Psalm 37:25

I was young and now I am old,
yet I have never seen the
righteous forsaken
or their children
begging bread.
NIV

Also Highlight; Psalm 37:23-24 & Psalm 37:39

Date:__/__/____

Insight

Through the peaks and troughs of life God calls us to put our trust wholly in Him. Being patient during the waiting period is fundamental as God assures us that He shall never forsake His righteous. Therefore, let us commit all our ways to Him.

Prayer Requests

Declare & Decree

1. I will delight myself in the Lord during my waiting period.
2. I trust wholly in God to fulfill my desires and petitions.
3. God grant me divine stillness & patience as I wait on You.
4. Order my steps O Lord, that You may delight in my ways.

Notes/Testimonies

A Prayer when Suffering Consequences of Sin

Psalm 38:9

All my longings lie open before
You, Lord;
my sighing is not hidden
from You.
NIV

Also Highlight; Psalm 38:1-3

Date:__/__/____

Insight

John 9:2 confirms that sometimes our afflictions are as a result of sin. Remember that the wages of sin is death (Rom 6:23). As our father, God has the right to discipline us (Heb 12:6). We ought to plead with our just God for mercy & forgiveness.

Prayer Requests

Declare & Decree

1. In Your wrath Lord, remember mercy!
2. Forgive me for all my transgressions & for those of the generations before me that are yet to be atoned for.
3. Make haste to help me O Lord of my salvation.

Notes/Testimonies

A Prayer for the Gift of Wisdom

Psalm 39:5

You have made my days a mere handbreadth;
the span of my years is as nothing before You.
Everyone is but a breath, even those who seem secure.
NIV

Also Highlight; Psalm 39:1 & Psalm 39:11

Date:__/__/____

Insight

Wisdom is mentioned as the first gift of the Holy Spirit, (1 Cor 12:7-11). We cannot always help who we have to interact with in our day to day but we can control what we say. The Holy Spirit can guide us on what to say in difficult situations.

Prayer Requests

Declare & Decree

1. Holy Spirit bless me with the gift of wisdom in abundance!
2. Lord help me muzzle my mouth when among the wicked that I shall not sin against You with my tongue.
3. Save me from my iniquities and spare me from Your rebuke!

Notes/Testimonies

Looking up to God for Help

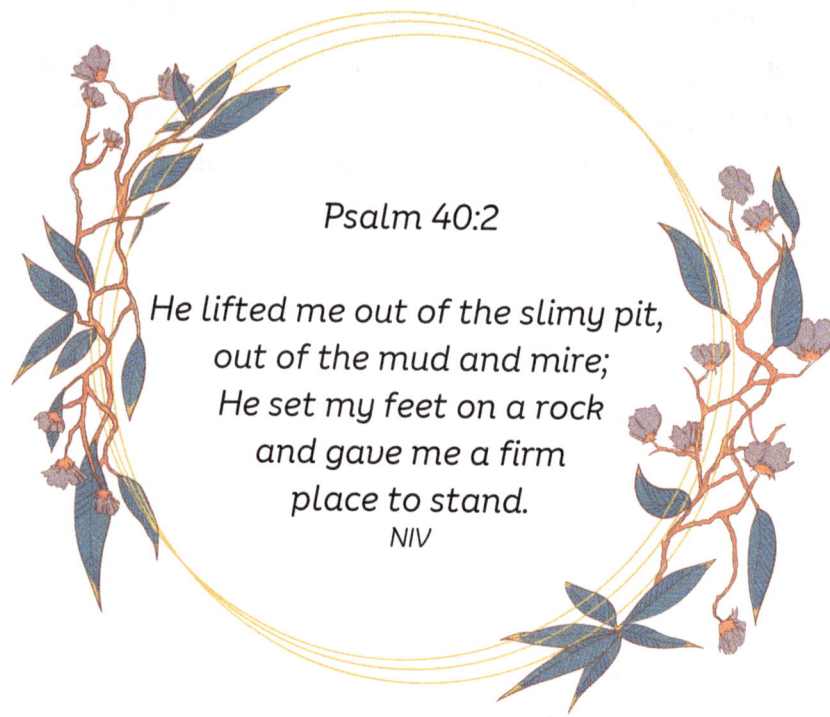

Psalm 40:2

He lifted me out of the slimy pit,
out of the mud and mire;
He set my feet on a rock
and gave me a firm
place to stand.
NIV

Also Highlight; Psalm 40:1 & Psalm 40:3

Date:__/__/____

Insight

King David says that he waited 'patiently' for the Lord's rescue & the Lord heard him. Patience while awaiting God's refuge as opposed to looking for other ways out shows that we trust in His saving grace. His salvation for the righteous is assured.

Prayer Requests

Declare & Decree

1. Lord I only look up to You the blessed hope of my salvation.
2. Pull me out of this muddy pit & set my feet on a steady rock.
3. Write Your law in my heart that I may do Your will Lord.
4. I will testify of Your goodness & Your tender mercies Oh Lord.

Notes/Testimonies

The Lord My Ever-Present Help

Psalm 46:5

God is within her, she will not fall;
God will help her at break of day.
NIV

Also Highlight; Psalm 46:1 & Psalm 46:10

Date:__/__/____

Insight

Fear is a common emotion to feel when facing life's challenges However, God has freed us from succumbing to it through the assurance that He is a very present help in the day of trouble. When life causes us to shake, He is our anchor to the ground.

Prayer Requests

Declare & Decree

1. For God is within me, I will not fall!
2. Lord You're my stronghold, my refuge & my high tower.
3. I choose to be still & wholly surrender all my fears to God.
4. His name is Emmanuel meaning Jesus is with me.

Notes/Testimonies

A Prayer for Pardon from Sin

Psalm 51:11-12

Do not cast me from Your
presence or take Your
Holy Spirit from me.
Restore to me the joy
of Your salvation
and grant me a willing
spirit, to sustain me.
NIV

Also Highlight; Psalm 51:10 & Psalm 51:17

Date:__/__/____

Insight

Since the first fall of man Adam, sin & death entered the world. We're all born with a sinful nature which is why to enter heaven & spend eternity with God we need to be born again (John 3:3). God is able to renew our mind, body & soul to reflect Him.

Prayer Requests

Declare & Decree

Lord Jesus, I admit that I am a sinner appointed rightfully for wrath due to my iniquities. I ask that You may wash me clean with Your precious blood that You shed on the cross for me. I invite You to come & live in my heart both now & forever Amen.

Notes/Testimonies

The Lord Faithfully Upholds Me

Psalm 54:4

Behold, God is my helper and ally;
The Lord is the sustainer of my soul [my upholder].
AMP

Also Highlight; Psalm 54:2 & Psalm 54:6

Date:__/__/____

Insight

Ebenezer is a Hebrew name of God meaning 'stone of help'. We need to learn to rest on Him as our rock. With God by our side, victory is always guaranteed despite the circumstance. When He delivers us, we should always give Him a sacrifice of praise.

Prayer Requests

Declare & Decree

1. Hear my prayer O God; Listen to the words of my mouth.
2. You are Ebenezer (my stone of help); only You are my helper.
3. I will offer to You a genuine sacrifice of praise & thanksgiving for You have delivered & saved me.

Notes/Testimonies

Fully Trusting in God who is Invincible to Man

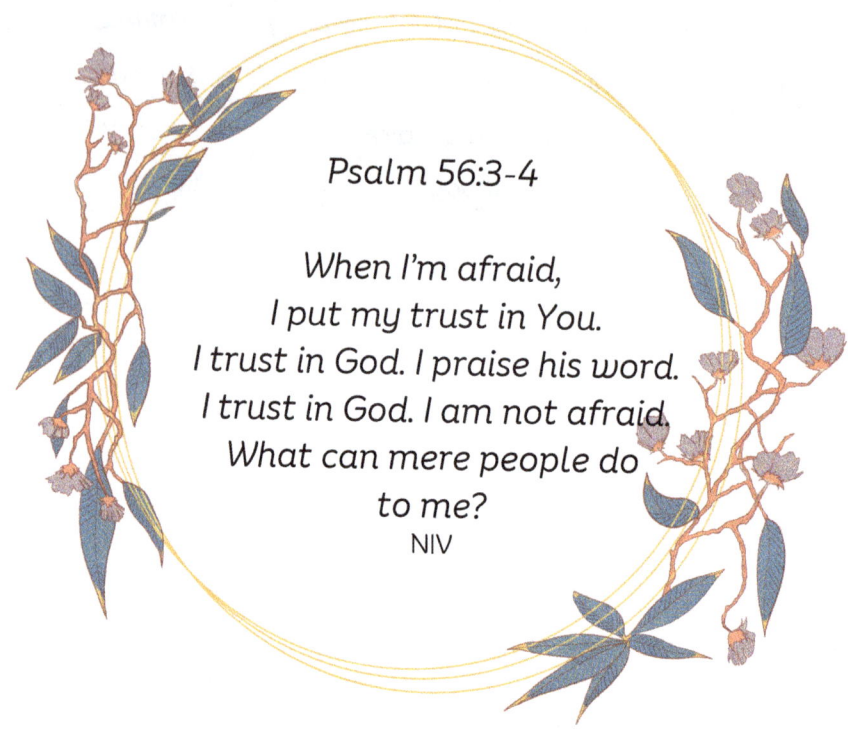

Psalm 56:3-4

When I'm afraid,
I put my trust in You.
I trust in God. I praise his word.
I trust in God. I am not afraid.
What can mere people do
to me?
NIV

Also Highlight; Psalm 56:9

Date:__/__/____

Insight

"Who are you that you fear mere mortals; human beings who are like grass?" (Isa. 51:12). The Lord has His hand over us & He will certainly not sit back & watch us walk into destruction. We should not live in fear of what men can do when God is with us.

Prayer Requests

Declare & Decree

1. God did not give me a spirit of fear but of power, love & a sound mind. I will therefore not live in fear of anyone.
2. I will leave vengeance to the Lord, the fighter of my battles.
3. I give You my offering of thanks for You have defended me.

Notes/Testimonies

Confidence in the Lord My Refuge

Psalm 61:2

From the ends of the earth I call
to You,
I call as my heart grows faint;
lead me to the rock that
is higher than I.
NIV

Also Highlight; Psalm 61:3-4

Date: __/__/____

Insight

Throughout scripture God is referred to as being a rock. This reflects His strength and stature which is solid. He is a strong refuge & a shield against evil works. The name of the Lord is a strong tower, the righteous run to it & are safe (Prov 18:10).

Prayer Requests

Declare & Decree

1. When my heart grows faint Lord, lead me to the rock that is higher than I.
2. Fight for me Lord, against all foes in pursuit of my life!
3. I will dwell in Your tent & in the shelter of Your wings, Lord.

Notes/Testimonies

A Prayer for Deliverance from Evil Traps and Snares

Psalm 64:7-8

But God will shoot them
with His arrows;
they will suddenly be
struck down.
He will turn their own
tongues against them
and bring them to ruin;
NIV

Also Highlight; Psalm 64:2-3

Date:__/__/____

Insight

In this chapter of Psalm, David highlights that wicked people have secret conspiracies and snares awaiting to trap the innocent. He reveals that the heart of a man is mysterious. However, God will shoot at them with an unexpected arrow.

Prayer Requests

Declare & Decree

1. Jehovah Magen, my shield & my refuge hide me against every wicked person monitoring me for an attack.
2. Let the wicked who lay traps before me fall in them instead!
3. Oh God of justice! Judge my case and arise to my salvation!

Notes/Testimonies

The Favour of the Lord is Abundant

Psalm 65:9

You care for the land and water it; You enrich it abundantly. The streams of God are filled with water to provide the people with grain, for so You have ordained it.
NIV

Also Highlight; Psalm 65:4 & Psalm 65:11

Date:__/__/____

Insight

Knowing Christ is a privilege. Scores of people pass through life without ever experiencing Jesus. It is a blessing to have God consider us His children through having faith in His son Jesus. Salvation is the greatest evidence of God's favour in our lives.

Prayer Requests

Declare & Decree

1. Thank You Lord for choosing to draw me near that I may dwell in Your courts.
2. Thank You for the gift of salvation through faith in Jesus!
3. I receive a harvest of abundance in my life in Jesus name!

Notes/Testimonies

The Results of Wickedness Versus Righteousness

Psalm 73:23-24

I am continually with You;
You have taken hold of my right hand.
You will guide me with Your counsel,
And afterward receive me to honour and glory.
NASB

Also Highlight; Psalm 73:18-19 & Psalm 73:26

Date:__/__/____

Insight

As believers who walk in righteousness we sometimes wonder why the wicked prosper. We might even find ourselves being envious of their lifestyles. However, their end is sure of a sudden destruction while the faithful will receive honour & glory.

Prayer Requests

Declare & Decree

1. Oh Lord forgive me for when I have submitted to carnality & been envious of the wicked and their ways.
2. Guide me with Your counsel Lord & receive me to honour!
3. I have made the Lord my refuge & my trust is placed in Him.

Notes/Testimonies

The Lord is Glorious in Power

Psalm 76:8-9

You caused judgment to be
heard from heaven;
The earth feared and was still,
When God arose to judgment,
To deliver all the oppressed
of the earth.
NKJV

Also Highlight; Psalm 76:4 & Psalm 76:11

Date:__/__/____

Insight

El Shaddai is a Hebrew name of God meaning 'God Almighty'. As Christians we need to remember that the battle is not ours but the Lords. In His justice, He promises to fight for us. We only need to be still & yield to His glorious power.

Prayer Requests

Declare & Decree

1. No weapon formed against me shall prosper & every tongue that rises against me let it be condemned!
2. Oh Lord I shall await Your fair judgement on my behalf.
3. The fear of the Lord is the beginning of wisdom.

Notes/Testimonies

The Lord's Victorious Track Record

Psalm 77:11-12

*I will remember the works of the Lord;
Surely I will remember Your wonders of old.
I will also meditate on all Your work,
And talk of Your deeds.*
NKJV

Also Highlight; Psalm 77:7-9

Date:__/__/____

Insight

God does not need to prove Himself. He is the I AM. He has performed great deeds & wonders since the days of old until today. When life inclines us to feel like our trust in God is in vain, we should remember how far He has brought us.

Prayer Requests

Declare & Decree

1. Lord, may Your right hand not change to be against me.
2. Thank You, Lord for this far You have brought me & that You will never leave me nor forsake me.
3. Your ways are higher than my ways, Lord I trust in You!

Notes/Testimonies

Restore Me O Lord!

Psalm 80:7,14

*Restore us, O God of hosts;
Cause Your face to shine,
And we shall be saved!*

*Return, we beseech You,
O God of hosts;
Look down from heaven and
see, And visit this vine*
NKJV

Also Highlight; Psalm 80:4-5

Date:__/__/____

Insight
In Joel 2:25 the Lord promises to restore the years the locust has eaten. After a period of judgement & punishment, God is able to restore glory & favour unto the repentant. He says that a broken & contrite heart He shall not despise (Psa. 51:17).

Prayer Requests

Declare & Decree
1. Restore me Lord! Cause Your countenance to shine upon me
2. Rare me as You would a vine & strengthen me for Yourself!
3. Lord, revive me & I will call on Your name.
4. I will not turn back from the Lord but abide in Him forever.

Notes/Testimonies

A Petition to Be Saved from Death

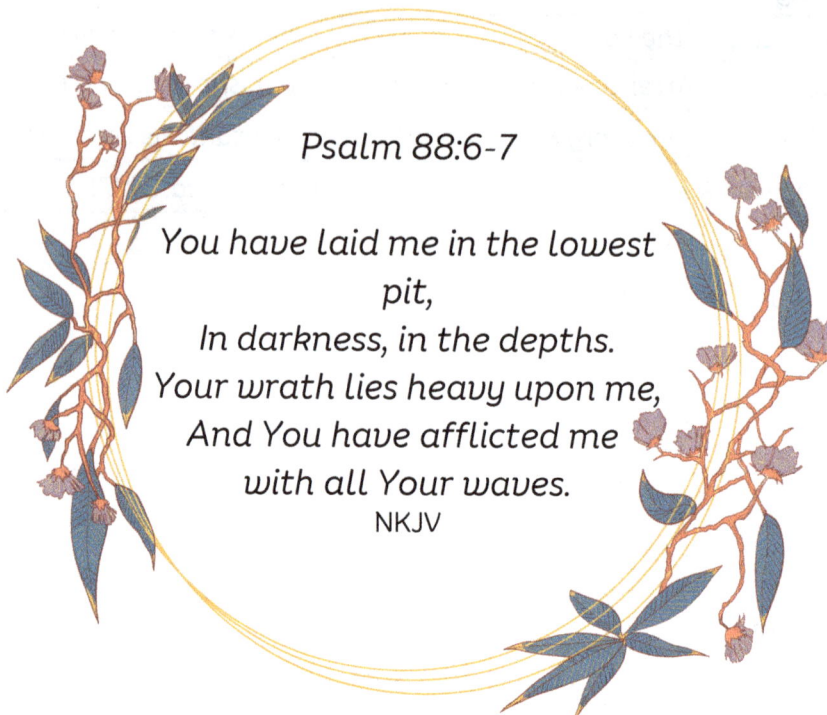

Psalm 88:6-7

You have laid me in the lowest pit,
In darkness, in the depths.
Your wrath lies heavy upon me,
And You have afflicted me
with all Your waves.
NKJV

Also Highlight; Psalm 88:2-3

Date:__/__/____

Insight

Some afflictions that plague us as a result of iniquity can result in an early death. If we find ourselves or others cast down, we we should petition for pardon from death. The enemy's agenda is to steal, kill & destroy but Jesus gives us life in abundance.

Prayer Requests

Declare & Decree

1. Show me mercy, Lord! Incline Your ear to my cry & hear me.
2. From a lowly place, I only look up for my salvation.
3. Do not reject my ask Lord, extend Your lovingkindness to me.
4. Use me as a sign of Your wonder in the land of the living,

Notes/Testimonies

A Man After God's Own Heart

Psalm 89:20-21

*I have found David My servant;
With My holy oil I have anointed him,
With whom My hand shall be established and steadfast;
My arm also shall strengthen him.*
AMP

Also Highlight; Psalm 89:1 & Psalm 89:49

Date:__/__/____

Insight

God called David a man after His own heart. Despite his great anointing, David was an imperfect man. He sinned against God when He killed Uriah & took his wife. But God had mercy on him & established an everlasting covenant with His servant David.

Prayer Requests

Declare & Decree

1. I let go of any bitterness, grudges & unforgiveness concealed in my heart. I command a release in the name of Jesus.
2. Soften my heart to show mercy to others Lord.
3. The Lord will show me the sure mercies of David.

Notes/Testimonies

God is the Alpha and the Omega

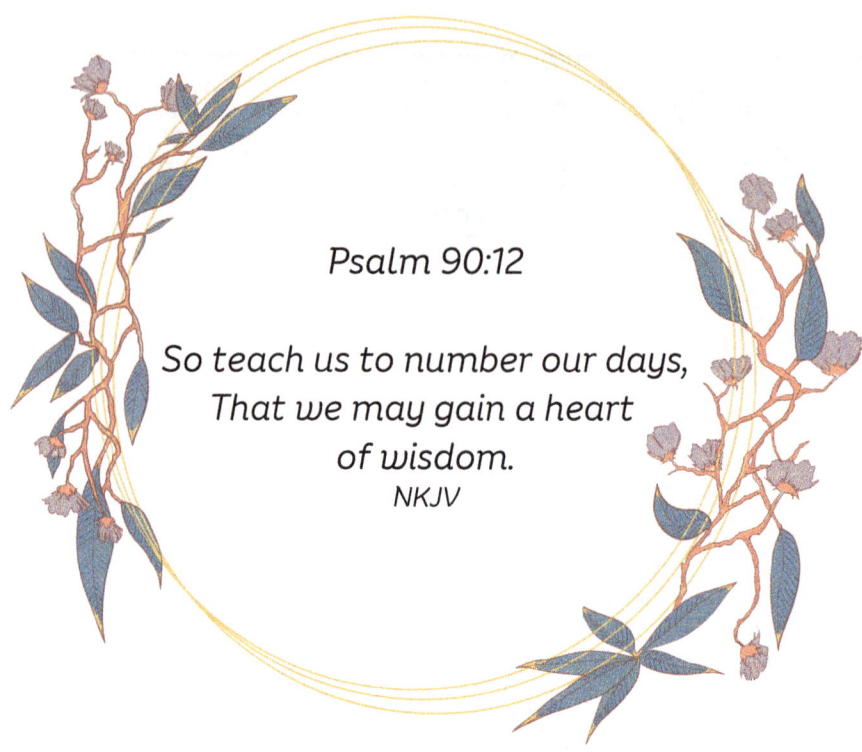

Psalm 90:12

So teach us to number our days,
That we may gain a heart
of wisdom.
NKJV

Also Highlight; Psalm 90:2-3 & Psalm 90:17

Date:__/__/____

Insight

God is the Alpha & the Omega, the beginning & the end. He existed when the earth was formless & desolate. He exists outside time as we know it. The first sin caused God to shorten our days on earth, the Lord compares our longevity to grass.

Prayer Requests

Declare & Decree

1. Lord You're the Alpha & Omega of my life.
2. Before I existed, You were, You formed me in my mother's womb. Therefore, I offer my life to You Lord.
3. Teach me to number my days Lord, that I may please You.

Notes/Testimonies

The Lord Almighty is My Shelter

Psalm 91:10-11

No evil shall befall you,
Nor shall any plague come near
your dwelling;
For He shall give His
angels charge over you,
To keep you in all your
ways.
NKJV

Also Highlight; Psalm 91:1-2 & Psalm 91:15-16

Date:__/__/____

Insight

The Lord is faithful, He strengthens us & protects us from the evil one (2 Thess. 3:3). We should always look up to God for His divine protection. He assures us safety under His pinions and promises salvation to His righteous now and forevermore.

Prayer Requests

Declare & Decree

1. The Lord is my refuge & my fortress, my God in whom I trust.
2. I will not fear terror, pestilence & arrows from the enemy.
3. No disaster will come near me nor my family in Jesus name!
4. Lord, send Your angels to watch over me at all times.

Notes/Testimonies

Praise the Lord for His Lovingkindness

Psalm 92:12-13

The righteous shall flourish like a palm tree,
He shall grow like a cedar in Lebanon.
Those who are planted in the house of the Lord
Shall flourish in the courts of our God.
NKJV

Also Highlight; Psalm 92:1-2 & Psalm 92:15

Date:__/__/____

Insight

Praise causes confusion in the enemy's camp (2 Chron 20:22). Give thanks to the Lord, for His lovingkindess endures forever. In the midst of anxiety and chaos, we should sing our praises to God. Let us never allow the enemy to steal our peace & joy.

Prayer Requests

Declare & Decree

1. Thank You Lord, for Your lovingkindness endures forever.
2. The Lord has done great things, praise His Holy Name!
3. Make me righteous in Your sight Oh Lord, that I will dwell in Your courts declaring Your everlasting faithfulness.

Notes/Testimonies

Vengeance belongs to the Lord

Psalm 94:12

Blessed is the man whom You discipline
and instruct, Lord,
And whom You teach
from Your law,
NASB

Also Highlight; Psalm 94:1 & Psalm 94:17-18

Date:__/__/____

Insight

The Lord is full and mercy and kindness for His righteous but He considers the wicked to be His own enemies. God is slow to anger & gives chances for repentance. But to the stubborn in their wickedness, He guarantees their destruction.

Prayer Requests

Declare & Decree

1. Lord I will await on You to execute Judgement on my behalf.
2. Soften my heart Lord, to receive Your instruction & discipline.
3. As I await You Lord, grant me peace in the midst of adversity.
4. May my heart always delight in the comfort of the Lord.

Notes/Testimonies

Jehovah, You are the Most High

Psalm 97:5-6

The mountains melt like wax
at the presence of the Lord,
At the presence of the Lord of
the whole earth.
The heavens declare His
righteousness,
And all the peoples
see His glory.
NKJV

Also Highlight; Psalm 97:1 & Psalm 97:1

Date:__/__/____

Insight

The Lord sits on His throne of righteousness and justice in Heaven as creation acknowledges His might as the creator. All other gods are false gods made by the hands & minds of man. The I AM cannot share His glory with them.

Prayer Requests

Declare & Decree

1. Thank You Lord for revealing Yourself to me that I may Praise You with deep revelation of who You are.
2. All creation declares that You Oh Lord, are King!
3. You protect the soul of the godly & save us from the wicked.

Notes/Testimonies

Start with a Grateful Heart

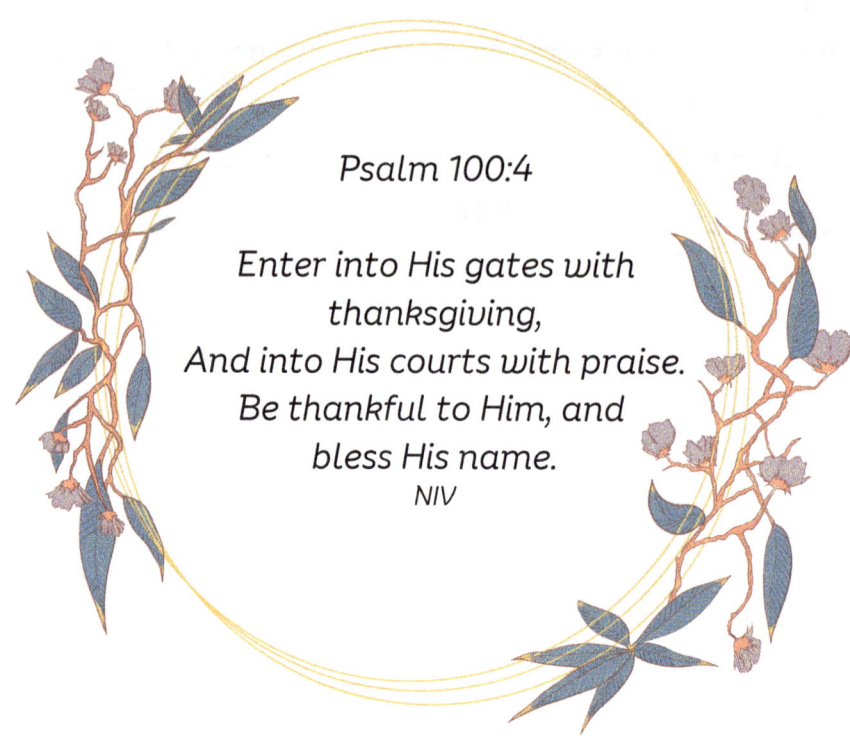

Psalm 100:4

Enter into His gates with thanksgiving,
And into His courts with praise.
Be thankful to Him, and
bless His name.
NIV

Also Highlight; Psalm 100:1-3 & Psalm 100:5

Date:__/__/____

Insight

Make a joyful sound unto Your Maker! Get into a praise break & give Him His due glory! We are often too keen on presenting our requests to God that we forget to start our prayers with gratitude. Let us always be grateful to God for He is good.

Prayer Requests

Declare & Decree

1. I repent for any ingratitude Lord, forgive me for all the times that I have borne an ungrateful spirit.
2. Thank You so much Lord Jesus, I praise Your Holy Name!
3. You're good and Your mercies are forever Lord.

Notes/Testimonies

The Lord Shall Arise to My Cause

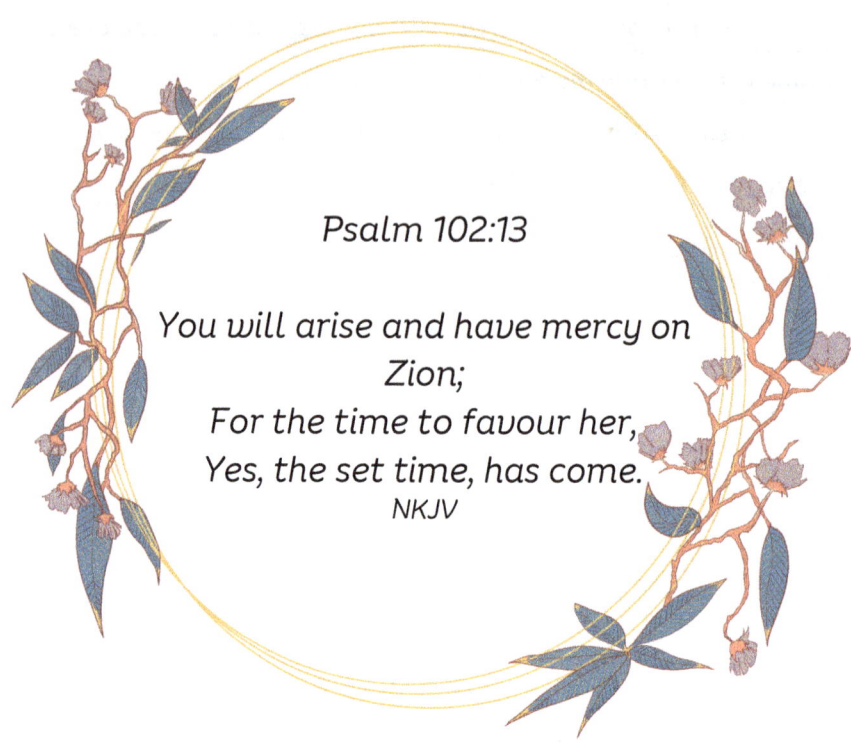

Psalm 102:13

You will arise and have mercy on Zion;
For the time to favour her,
Yes, the set time, has come.
NKJV

Also Highlight; Psalm 102:19-20 & Psalm 102:245

Date: __/__/____

Insight

Though weeping endures for a night, joy will always come in the morning (Psa. 30:5). Though the consequences of sin may be quite hard to endure, we should not despair but plead for God's unwavering mercy as He is compassionate in nature.

Prayer Requests

Declare & Decree

1. Incline Your ear to me Lord, & answer me when I call on You.
2. For my cause Lord, You will arise & have compassion on me as it is the appointed time to be gracious & show favour to me.
3. Restore me Lord, that I may live the full length of my days.

Notes/ Testimonies

The Lord's Everlasting Mercy

Psalm 103:11-12

For as high as the heavens are
above the earth,
So great is His mercy toward
those who fear Him.
As far as the east is from the
west,
So far has He removed our
wrongdoings from us.
NASB

Also Highlight; Psalm 103:1 & Psalm 103:17

Date:__/__/____

Insight

It is very easy to feel entitled to God's enduring mercies that we forget to thank Him for showing it to us. It is important not to take advantage of God's merciful nature as it is undeserved & accorded to us only by His grace.

Prayer Requests

Declare & Decree

1. All that is within me praises You Lord Jesus!
2. I thank You Lord for You are merciful & gracious.
3. I am grateful Lord for You haven't dealt with me as I deserve but have completely separated me from my transgressions.

Notes/Testimonies

God's Covenant with Abraham to Generations

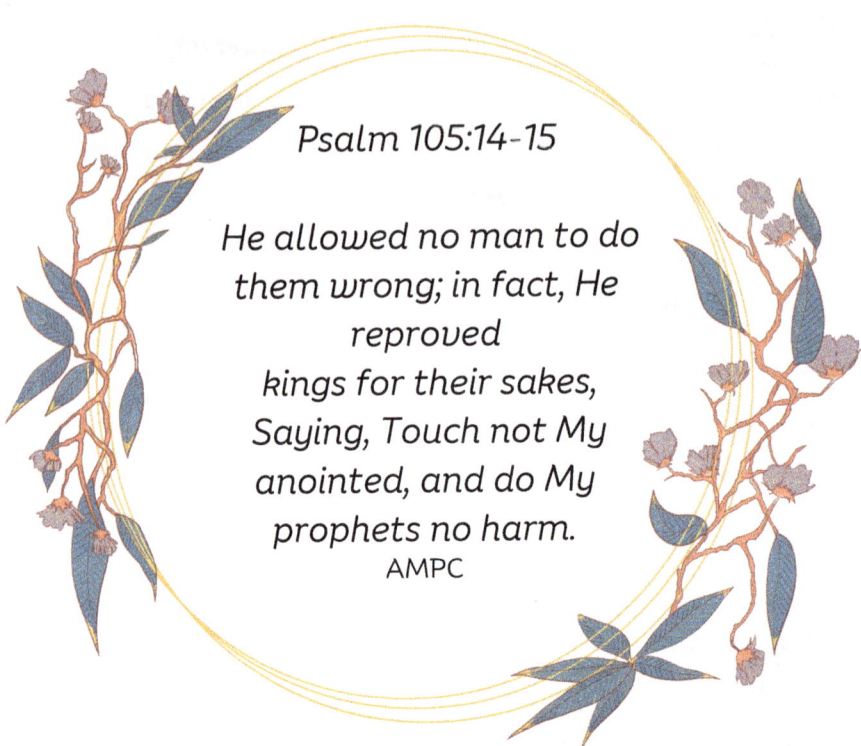

Psalm 105:14-15

He allowed no man to do them wrong; in fact, He reproved
kings for their sakes, Saying, Touch not My anointed, and do My prophets no harm.
AMPC

Also Highlight; Psalm 105:8 & Psalm 105:42-43

Date:__/__/____

Insight

Thousands of years ago, the Lord made a covenant with Abraham whom He also calls His friend. The promise initially meant only for Israelites has now been extended to all Gentiles & through our belief in Christ Jesus we're also kingdom heirs.

Prayer Requests

Declare & Decree

1. The Lord says over me "touch not my anointed one!"
2. For my sake Lord, You will rebuke kings & allow no man to oppress me.
3. Thank You for You will bring me out with a joyful shout.

Notes/Testimonies

Man's Rebellion and the Lord's Faithfulness

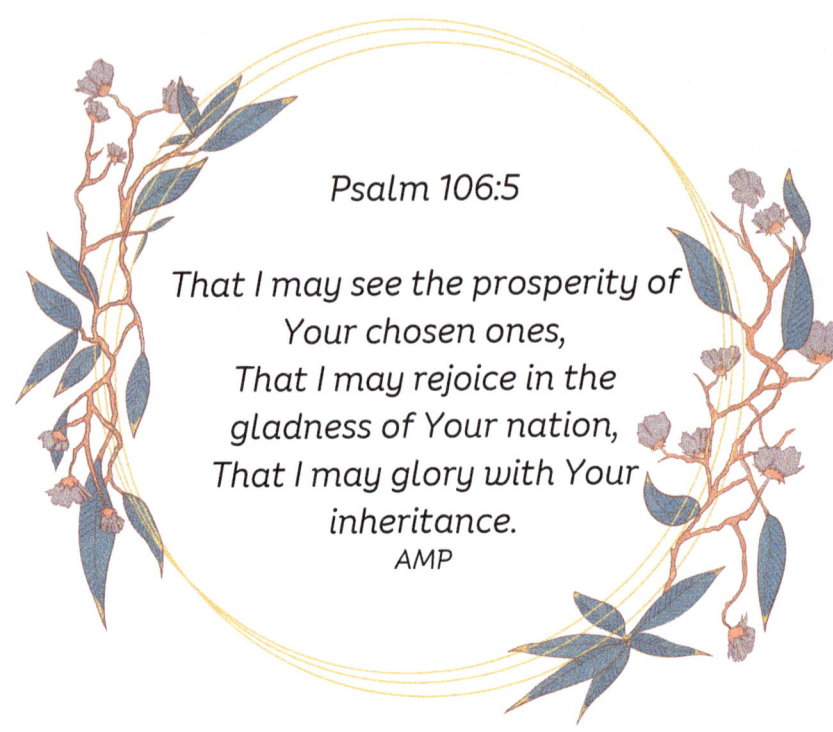

Psalm 106:5

That I may see the prosperity of
Your chosen ones,
That I may rejoice in the
gladness of Your nation,
That I may glory with Your
inheritance.
AMP

Also Highlight; Psalm 106:1 & Psalm 106:7-8

Date:__/__/____

Insight

Despite all the miracles the Lord did for the Israelites in the 400 years in the desert from Egypt to Canaan, they were often quick to rebel against Him. Sometimes we also forget how far the Lord has brought us & let rebellion sip into our hearts.

Prayer Requests

Declare & Decree

1. Forgive me Lord for all the times I have forgotten Your faithfulness and let my sorrow cause me to rebel against You.
2. Thank You for rescinding my sentence & showing me love.
3. Blessed be the God of Israel from everlasting Amen!

Notes/Testimonies

Thanksgiving for Deliverance

Psalm 107:15-16

Let them give thanks to the
Lord for His lovingkindness,
And for His wonderful acts to
the children of men!
For He has shattered the gates
of bronze
And cut the bars of
iron apart.
AMP

Also Highlight; Psalm 107:6 & Psalm 107:20

Date:__/__/____

Insight

Give thanks to the Lord for He came to your salvation. You cried out to God in your trouble & He rescued you from your affliction. He sent forth His word and healed your situation. God is faithful, & He will surely do it again.

Prayer Requests

Declare & Decree

1. Thank You Lord for You always rescue & deliver me.
2. The Lord has broken the gates of bronze & cut the iron bars causing bondage & limitation in my life in Jesus name!
3. The Lord has secured my feet high & away from affliction.

Notes/Testimonies

Humility Precedes Honour

Psalm 113:8

*That He may seat him with princes—
With the princes of His people.*
AMP

Also Highlight; Psalm 113:7 & Psalm 113:9

Date:__/__/____

Insight

The Lord opposes the proud but gives grace to the humble (Prov. 29:23). Humility is equated to the fear of the Lord its wages are riches, honour & life. Let us ask for God to break whatever is in us that causes pride & to grace us with humility.

Prayer Requests

Declare & Decree

1. Lord, any Leviathan spirit that causes me to have a prideful heart I ask that You break it in Jesus mighty name.
2. I declare freedom from the pride of life & walk into humility.
3. Thank You Lord for You will elevate me to sit with princes.

Notes/Testimonies

Thanksgiving for Mercy

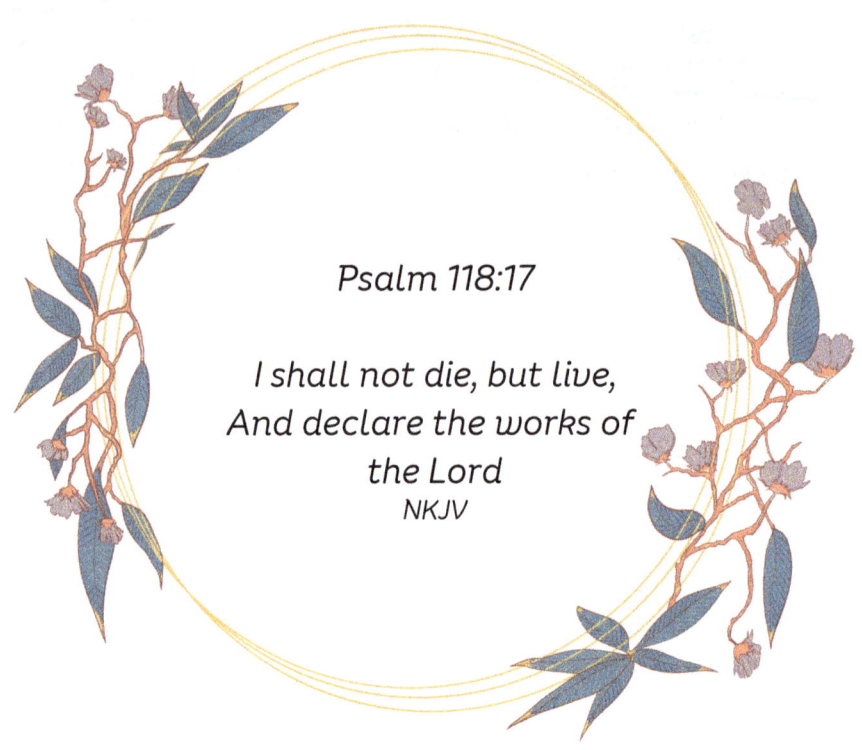

Psalm 118:17

*I shall not die, but live,
And declare the works of
the Lord*
NKJV

Also Highlight; Psalm 118:8 & Psalm 118:22-23

Date:__/__/____

Insight

Paul in Romans reminds us that if the Lord is for us then who dare be against us? The Lord is the lifter up of our heads (Psa. 3:3). When cast down by your situation or the people around you, remember the Lord will uplift you in due time.

Prayer Requests

Declare & Decree

1. My confidence is in You Lord the lifter up of my head.
2. I declare that I will not die but live to declare the works of the Lord in the land of the living.
3. Thank You Lord for all the marvellous works You have done.

Notes/Testimonies

Meditating on the Law of God

Psalm 119:36-37

Help me want to obey Your rules instead of selfishly wanting riches. Turn my eyes from looking at vanities; give me life in Your ways.
ICB

Also Highlight; Psalm 119:9 & Psalm 119:71-72

Date:__/__/____

Insight

Without experiencing the troughs of life, we would never fully appreciate the peaks of life. Our deliverances put a word of testimony on our lips. We shouldn't lust over riches for selfish gain but yearn for Jesus who is worth much more than gold.

Prayer Requests

Declare & Decree

1. I will meditate on Your word day & night Lord, that You will engrave Your law in the depths of my heart.
2. Open my eyes to the spiritual truth in Your word, Lord.
3. Lord, purge out of me that which distracts me from You.

Notes/Testimonies

The Lord is on Guard

Psalm 121:3-4

*He will not allow your foot to be moved;
He who keeps you will not slumber.
Behold, He who keeps Israel Shall neither slumber nor sleep.*
(NKJV)

Also Highlight; Psalm 121:1

Date:__/__/____

Insight

Psalm 121 assures us that God is always watching over those that seek Him. The Lord doesn't get tired or take breaks from His throne. He keeps His righteous far away from the perils of the enemy. Claim His 24-hour protection over your life.

Prayer Requests

Declare & Decree

1. Thank You Lord for You're Ebenezer; my Helper.
2. The Lord is my keeper & shade on my right hand.
3. The sun shall not harm me by day nor the moon by night.
4. The Lord protects my going out & my coming in.

Notes/Testimonies

The Lord Provides an Escape

Psalm 124:7-8

*We have escaped like a bird from the snare of the fowlers; The trap is broken and we have escaped.
Our help is in the name of the Lord, Who made heaven and earth.*
AMP

Also Highlight; Psalm 124:2-3

Date:__/__/____

Insight

The Lord has hidden & protected us from the wrath of our enemies & those that have come against us through the years. The enemy may have caused us to feel backed up against the wall but the Lord always provides a way of divine escape.

Prayer Requests

Declare & Decree

1. The Lord is always on my side. He is mine & I am His.
2. The Lord will not give me to prey to be torn by their teeth,
3. The fowlers' snare is broken & my soul has escaped!
4. My help is in the name of the Lord.

Notes/Testimonies

True Prosperity is from the Lord

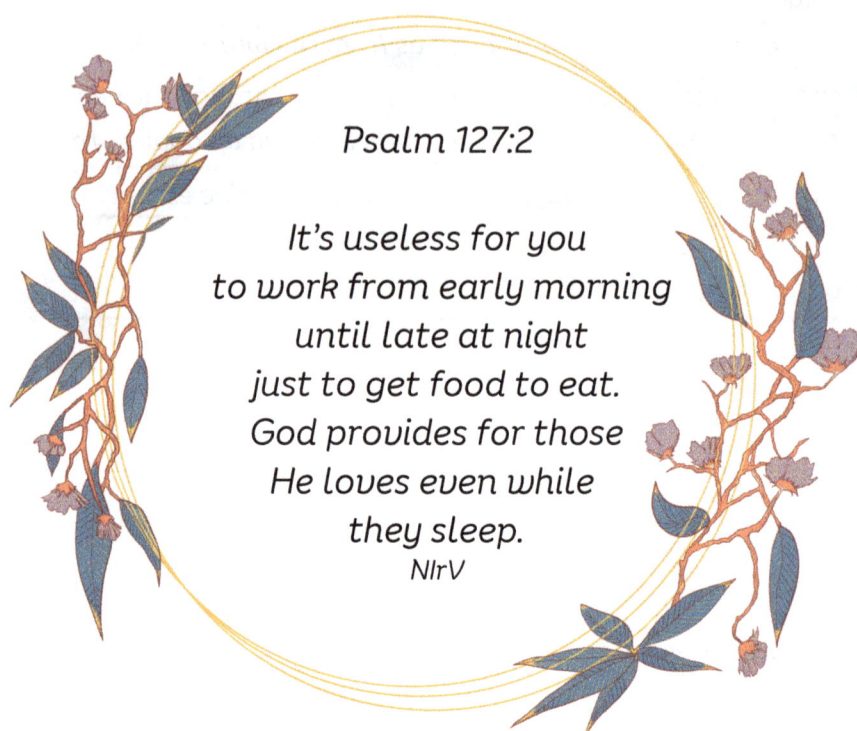

Psalm 127:2

It's useless for you
to work from early morning
until late at night
just to get food to eat.
God provides for those
He loves even while
they sleep.
NIrV

Also Highlight; Psalm 127:1

Date:__/__/____

Insight

It's not by might nor by power but by the Spirit of the Lord (Zech. 4:6). Everything done in our own understanding is vain. Let us always trust in the Lord with all our hearts & lean not on our own understanding but acknowledge Him in all our ways.

Prayer Requests

Declare & Decree

1. Lord please always guide & direct my steps. Teach me to walk in Your Spirit at all times.
2. Jesus is taking care and looking after me daily.
3. The Lord is involved in the works of my hands.

Notes/Testimonies

Our Omnipresent and Omniscient God

Psalm 139:7-8

Where can I go from Your Spirit?
Or where can I flee from Your presence?
If I ascend into heaven, You are there;
If I make my bed in hell, behold, You are there.
NKJV

Also Highlight; Psalm 139:16 & Psalm 139:24

Date:__/__/____

Insight

Omnipresent means God is everywhere & Omniscient means He is all-knowing. Before God formed us in our mothers' wombs He knew us & set us apart (Jer 1:5). We cannot run away from God's presence. He holds us securely in the palm of His hands.

Prayer Requests

Declare & Decree

1. Lord, You alone know my end from my beginning.
2. The Lord is a hedge behind and before me.
3. I thank You Lord for I am fearfully & wonderfully made.
4. Search me for any wickedness & replace it with eternal life.

Notes/Testimonies

A Prayer for Safety from Evil Works

Psalm 141:5

Let the righteous strike me;
It shall be a kindness.
And let him rebuke me;
It shall be as excellent oil;
Let my head not refuse it.
NKJV

Also Highlight; Psalm 141:4 & Psalm 141:9

Date:___/___/_____

Insight

As believers in Christ, our daily walk in the Spirit consecrates us & separates us from wicked counsels. Our company also changes to be of those walking in righteousness. As we march onto Zion, the wicked await their divine judgement from God.

Prayer Requests

Declare & Decree

1. Set a guard, O Lord, over my mouth; keep watch over my lips.
2. Separate me from wicked counsels & plant my feet in the company of the righteous, O Lord Jesus.
3. Give me a heart that receives righteous correction & rebuke.

Notes/Testimonies

A Prayer for Deliverance and Consecration

Psalm 143:10

Teach me to do Your will,
For You are my God;
Your Spirit is good.
Lead me in the land of uprightness.
NKJV

Also highlight; Psalm 143:8 & Psalm 143:11

Date:__/__/____

Insight

As believers in Christ, our daily walk in the Spirit consecrates us & separates us from wicked counsels. Our company also changes to be of those walking in righteousness. As we march onto Zion, the wicked await their divine judgement from God.

Prayer Requests

Declare & Decree

1. Set a guard, O Lord, over my mouth; keep watch over my lips.
2. Separate me from wicked counsels & plant my feet in the company of the righteous, Lord Jesus.
4. Give me a heart that receives righteous correction & rebuke.

Notes/Testimonies

The Lord's Majestic and Loving Nature

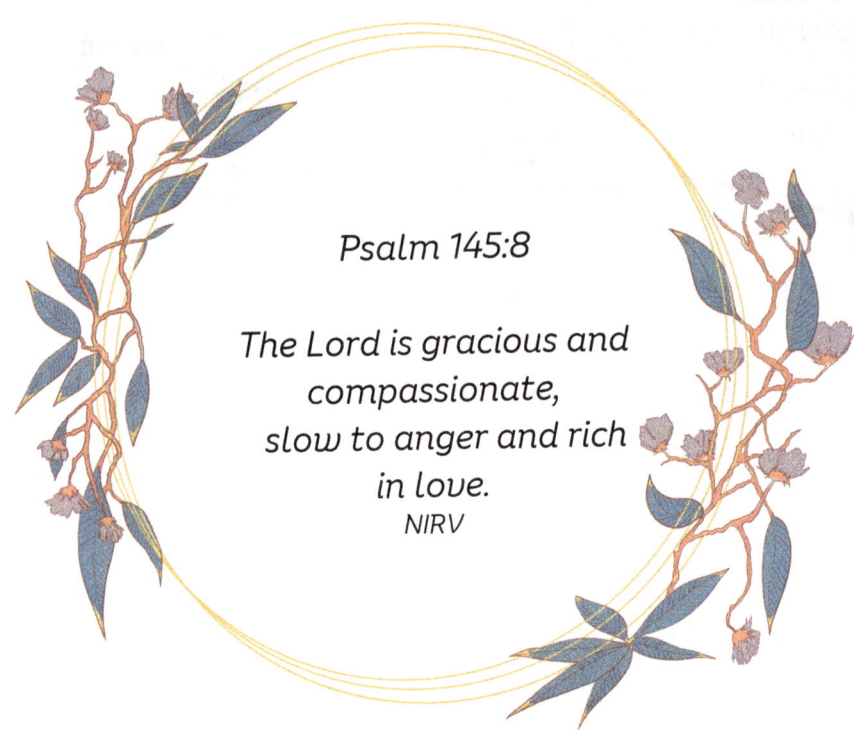

Psalm 145:8

The Lord is gracious and
compassionate,
slow to anger and rich
in love.
NIRV

Also highlight; Psalm 145:5 & Psalm 145:18

Date:__/__/____

Insight

The Lord is full of grace & love, He understands that our imperfect nature causes us to fall short of His glory. This does not permit us an abuse of His grace but testifies of His nature. Our mouths should continually speak the praise of the Lord.

Prayer Requests

Declare & Decree

1. Great is the Lord who is greatly to be praised.
2. O Lord, do it for me that I may tell of Your mighty works.
3. The Lord is good & full of tender mercies towards me.
4. The Lord is near to me for I call unto Him in truth.

Notes/Testimonies

A Song of Praise to the Lord

Psalm 150:6

Let everything that has breath
praise the Lord.
Praise the Lord.
NIRV

Also highlight; Psalm 150:2 & Psalm 150:4

Date: __/__/____

Insight

The Psalm ends with this victorious chapter. This is also your testimony in Jesus name! You're coming out of your situations a victor & not a victim, above only & never beneath. The Lord has heard your cry & will rescue you. All praises due to Him!

Prayer Requests

Declare & Decree

1. I will praise God in His sanctuary!
2. I will praise Him in the heavenlies!
3. I will praise Him in His mighty & excellent works!
4. Let everything that has breath, PRAISE THE LORD!

Notes/Testimonies

Notes

Notes

Notes

Notes

Notes

Notes

For all resources related to ministry; including to Give or connect on social media, Scan the Linktree QR Code below using your rear-facing camera.

https://linktr.ee/consecrated_

www.ingramcontent.com/pod-product-compliance
Lightning Source LLC
Chambersburg PA
CBHW071352160426
42811CB00095B/561